HAVE YOU HAD LUNCH?

SUSAN STEWART

authorHOUSE®

AuthorHouse™ UK Ltd.
500 Avebury Boulevard
Central Milton Keynes, MK9 2BE
www.authorhouse.co.uk
Phone: 08001974150

First published by AuthorHouse 3/22/2011

ISBN: 978-1-4567-7434-9 (sc)
ISBN: 978-1-4567-7433-2 (e)

I would like to thank Vicky for seeing something in my original idea, which gave me the confidence I needed. I would also like to say a big thank you to Mr Ian Hamerton, who gave up his time to put my work in to a logical perspective.

To Mrs Clare Beautyman, (Programme Manager Hairdressing) at Farnbourgh College of Technology. And Mr Doug Dimmack, (Head of Careers/Vocation Education) at Courtmoor Secondary School, Fleet Hampshire. Thank You for taking the time to read and endorse my work.

Mum, I Love You. I miss you

Pat. Friday's just aren't the same.

HAVE YOU HAD LUNCH?

*T*his is an insight into the world of an everyday hairdresser: a guide to what work as a 'Saturday Girl', an apprentice, a stylist and the manager of a successful salon is all about. For twenty-two years I have, like most tradesmen and women, gone about my day in a very busy and demanding way. To do well and become a *great* stylist you will need to work hard, both physically and mentally. The need to apply both of these demands is great if you intend to make something of your career and, by doing so, you will over the long term earn both respect and a creditable name for yourself in the industry. It is a world in which some of the most fascinating and creative, yet sometimes extremely repetitive, work takes place. Above all, it can be one of the most mentally challenging and physically demanding careers you could ever pursue.

WHEN I GROW UP I WANT TO BE…

"When I grow up I want to be a vet." Well at least that's what I thought until my mum quite rightly pointed out my great love for animals; how I never made it through 'Watership Down' without blubbing my heart out. And then there was Lassie, thank goodness she always pulled through if she ever suffered an injury! Even from a young age I couldn't bear to see animals suffering, so was this going to be the right career for me? It is true that 'mum always knows best' and, when she said I would spend my working life in tears, deep down I knew she was right.

Consequently, when I announced that I was going to be a hairdresser, it was with conviction, and I have never wavered from that decision.

Now, when I look back, I have a smile on my face as I recall one of my earliest memories as a stylist. "We want to play hairdressers!", was a phrase you would often hear as my parents settled down in front of the television for the evening; my mum indulging in her favourite T.V. soap or Murder Mystery. Both my sister and I regularly set up shop behind the sofa as we aimed to 'wash' her hair and massage her scalp. Unfortunately for my dad, mum hated people fiddling with her head: she would always say, "sorry girls, you know how much it fidgets me, can you do your father's hair instead? He won't mind." With that, we gathered up our equipment (a comb, a hairbrush and our imaginations) and attacked our dad's head. I'm not convinced that we displayed the best technique and we were most probably quite brutal in our approach. In fact, it wasn't until many years later that I learnt that brushing hair was always best carried out gently so as to minimise the risk of damage to the client's hair and scalp. As we were usually standing on tiptoes, that our hands or brush - (weapon) might actually reach Dad's head was a result and probably more of a physical blow than a therapeutic stroke! I'm sure that the massage would also have left a lot to be desired : it takes considerable time and practice to perfect such skills. Even on the evenings when we had an adequate platform to stand on and could reach our target more easily, the spider-like fingers trailing towards his eyebrows would have been a problem in the real world; all wet and covered in conditioner especially for those clients wearing a full face of make-up. I don't ever recall him complaining: maybe he felt he was outnumbered by three females so perhaps it was best just to let us get on with it for a quiet evening, or there was that slim chance that he actually enjoyed it?

Hairdressing is a career to which you may end up dedicating most of yourself, but for some clients that still will not be enough... Over the years, you may meet some truly great people and some may even become your friends. For most, if you provide your best, they will greatly value you and your skill; in time they may come to see you as almost 'godlike' or at least the creator of all things good for them, once every six weeks. A still smaller minority will steal your thunder and your ability to think straight; they will rob you of your confidence and leave you feeling totally worthless! For the fifty to sixty clients you will encounter during a typical working week most will leave you feeling revitalised and completely satisfied. It will be that one error or misinterpretation during a consultation that you will remember for the rest of the day, or longer if you do not accept that it's only human to err and move on! These little setbacks will hopefully be few and far between throughout your career and the best way to deal with them is to learn from them and then move on. The funniest thing about perhaps 90% of those situations is that such clients still always want you, and nobody else, to do their hair. As for the other 10%, by the end of the week you probably won't remember they exist until years down the line when you are reminiscing, or probably laughing over past experiences.

As time and you move forward, you will suddenly become aware of how your confidence has grown and your knowledge has increased tenfold. You will soon notice that Information is readily available to you in every degree, and every angle has been covered.

As in film, television, the music industry and the arts, hairdressing is not without its history and many great names will both guide and inspire you throughout your career. If you pay 'attention to detail' and take time to learn the important founding aspects, you won't go far wrong. Stylists such as Vidal Sassoon shaped the basics of every haircut: giving us the bob, a timeless classic worn by both men and women worldwide. He helped make us feel more classy, confident and desirable. Such things are known to most women; even if you are wearing your favourite dress, most coveted shoes and picture-perfect make-up, if our hair lets us down all we want to do is pull the duvet back over our heads and start again tomorrow!

Look around you, hair is everywhere! Accompanied by the right knowledge you do not have to venture far for inspiration: draw it from your client's lifestyle, what he or she does for a living, and how much time they have each day to recreate your masterpiece. Ask the relevant questions and then **LISTEN...**

THE APPRENTICE

*T*he phone started to ring. I looked around and as I was the only body on the shop floor, I paused for a moment before deciding to answer it. "Good morning", I remember saying "Can I help you?" It was a ladies voice and she went on to enquire if we sold vibrators…

That particular morning was the first of my two weeks' work experience, the thing you do in your second to last year of school and which is aimed at giving you some insight into the big world that follows formal education. I had been placed two floors up in the electrical department of my nearest large departmental store in a town not too far from where I lived. Looking back now it seems ridiculous that I applied to spend a week there, travelling back and forth by train, when it had no real connection twith the career path I really wanted to follow. I had only managed to get one of the weeks in a local salon near to my home as they already had another girl signed up at the time. I had heard the department store had a small hair and beauty salon so I applied to complete my first week there, but once I had arrived they thought it better to move me around daily to different departments as they presumed I would get bored.

But back to the 'phone call…As luck would have it my brain kicked into gear, 'this is a wind-up surely?' I thought to myself and so, with that thought in mind, I quickly replied,

"I'm not sure madam, it's my first day here and I'm new in electrics. A qualified member of staff should be back soon so if you would care to leave me your name and number I'll make sure someone returns your call."

With that, a few giggles and a round of applause, which appeared to develop from behind the counter at the back of the shop floor, my fellow colleagues trooped out one by one saying, 'well done, we were hoping you would have a sense of humour'… and I did. Practical jokes are very common in the work place so just laugh them off as harm is rarely meant. A colleague of mine once sent the new 'Saturday Girl' out to the local hardware store in order to buy her a new bubble for her flat topper and, when doing the lunch round, asked her to get a 'chicken lip and tomato' sandwich. It makes the staff laugh at the time and afterwards can seem a little mean, but these things happen to us all at some point and remember one day it will probably be you heading the wind up.

Week Two was already upon me and I was more than ready to find out what the future had in store for me. As I arrived, I could see two of the girls were already there busying themselves with their morning duties. One girl was rapidly mopping the large floor and another was following behind with a towel attached to a broom to mop up the excess water in order to make it 'client friendly'.

I was greeted momentarily by one of the girls and told to go out the back and make myself a cup of tea. As I made my way towards the rear of the salon into what was obviously the staff room I really did feel like the new girl, a fish totally out of water. It was the first occasion in a long time that I hadn't have a clue who anyone was or where anything was kept.

The staff knew my name and that I was there for work experience, but with just this little knowledge of me they had helped make me feel truly welcome. You do hear of people who turn up without anybody knowing who they are or indeed what to do with them. One of the girls asked if I could just hang on for a minute whilst they finished the floor and then we could put our feet-up together for a bit before the others started to roll-in. With that, the other girl bustled round from behind the basins muttering how one day the salon floor would be the death of her unless someone else ever took their turn in doing the drying! Her comments were dismissed instantly with a, "blah, blah, stop whingeing and meet Sue, she's signed-up for a week with Bible-Basher!" They suggested that I must be mad, but I was hoping to fit in well with everyone there.

As the girls started arriving for work everyone seemed nice and all greeted me with a, "hello my name is…", but I soon learnt that every morning would start differently. On some days 8.45 a.m. would be quite tranquil, when all was well on the emotional front. Then there were the mornings where lots of tears and comforting would herald the start of the day as someone's relationship had hit a slight blip, or huge boulder! On occasions it was simply a hive of activity, girls doing their hair and make-up or bustling in late.

The salon owner and, as things turned out, my boss for the next two years was on his way to the salon. The girls were keen to get me looking busy as Dan was due to arrive at any moment and his mood could never be predicted. As he was a religious man they put it down to how he and God were feeling at the start of each new day and how well they were getting on. A couple of the girls rolled their eyes and stood there with a 'how ridiculous' look on their faces and prompted me to grab a cloth and help polish the shelves. If there's one thing that Dan liked to see it was the staff looking busy and to be fair you could say this about any boss, anywhere. As a business man or woman you are always going to want things to look good and not just on paper so if you are intending to take hairdressing seriously you will have to get used to cleaning in a *big* way.

I appeared to click with all of the girls apart from one, who made me feel faintly uneasy and seemed to be watching my every move. After a few days I mentioned my misgivings to one of the girls who quickly put my mind at ease. She told me not to take any notice as it was just 'her way' and she was probably watching her competition; apparently Dan had not been happy with her work for a while and she clearly felt that I was after her job.

We cleaned the shelves and washed the basins until they shone. All the work stations and mirrors had been cleaned during the previous evening to reduce the morning's workload and the salon was now open and ready for the day ahead. Immediately I was asked whether I'd like to learn how to shampoo a client's hair, awkwardly I said, "yes". Now this can go fairly well, or really badly depending on how wet you get the client. For me, it went moderately well, but I did have one of their older clients to be my guinea pig and I could tell from the off she was a sweetie and would not have complained even if I had drenched her! Funnily enough I found washing a stranger's hair more daunting than my first haircut and I can only put this down to the the that fact it may be the first time you are in physical contact with a complete stranger without knowing how sensitive they may be. For example, one person may find the water too hot, yet another will tell you it is too cold; some clients will like you to be quite firm in your approach whereas others may scream at you to be more gentle. No matter what, no two people will be the same, so it's always best just to ask what they prefer before starting the procedure. I was bawled at several times by 'high maintenance divas' who, in most cases threw "you stupid girl" around the salon for all to hear. Back then when I was young and knew no different, like many others I would be left red-faced and feeling totally embarrassed with my confidence dented big time.

Two of the many great things to accompany age and experience are confidence and self worth; both of which I regret not having possessed as a teenager. I never failed to defend myself in a war of words with my parents, always determined to have the last word, but in a hectic salon situation for the best part of an hour when 'Mrs. 10.30 a.m. every Friday' was holding court by putting the 'new girl' through her induction I would often be rendered speechless. When this happens to you, as it will,, one of the many things you will have whispered in your ear will be, "don't take any notice of the old dragon, she does it to everyone!" These words are meant to help comfort you, but they won't stop you running out the back of the salon crying your eyes out. Welcome to the 'big wide world', a place where your mum is not the only one with a license to slap your legs...

These days, I would not allow someone to speak to me or a member of my team in such a manner. As manageress, I would need to find out

what was the cause of such a breakdown between the client and member of staff involved no matter what position they hold in the salon. Of course, anyone can make a mistake and this can't always be helped, but once someone has placed their hair and trust in your hands there really isn't much room for error. Fortunately, with age comes experience, a knowledgeable head can solve many a problem and most undesirable situations can be rectified there and then or at least over a few salon visits. I must confess that I have never followed my career by the dictum 'the customer is always right', as I do not believe that they are. However, with that said, if a situation should ever develop, I feel strongly that the customer must be made to feel totally comfortable, happy and in control while in my care and to appreciate that I would never compromise quality for expediency. Nevertheless, it does not give the client the right to speak to or treat an employee as if they were something the client had just found on the bottom of their shoe!

At the end of my week in the salon I knew without a doubt that hairdressing was for me; I loved everything I had seen take place around me and hoped to be part of it in the future. As I entered the salon for my final day, the girls told me that Dan had been really pleased with my efforts throughout the week and I was so pleased to hear this as I'd been hoping to put my name down in case a Saturday job become available. The girls encouraged me to go for it and when, just a few weeks later, I got the call offering me a job, I really couldn't believe it. In this way the road opened up into one of the biggest chapters of my life, WORK.

Don't ever be afraid to put yourself forward for something you really want to do, for if you don't someone else may get there before you and this could result in them having something which could have meant great things for you. Salons can only take on so many new trainees each year so get your name down as soon as possible. If you already have a Saturday job in a salon it could go greatly in your favour should you wish to proceed into an apprenticeship.

When visiting a hair salon many of us are only aware of the stylist, the person who cuts our hair. You would do well to be aware of the person who took your jacket, washed your hair, made your cup of tea and swept the floor around you, as one day if you love the idea of being that great stylist this will be you for a couple of years. Most professions require us to start at the very bottom and work our way up to where we want to be. In most salons you will spend a great deal of time standing, cleaning, shampooing, sweeping, running around after other people and observing before you even pick up a pair of scissors. Why? Because you don't know what you are doing, therefore you cannot be trusted with anything else.

After many weeks as a 'Saturday Girl' I suddenly received the devastating news that the salon no longer needed me, although I was told repeatedly that I had done nothing wrong and it was simply that the salon wasn't busy enough to warrant me working there for a while. I took comfort in telling myself that it would be great to have Saturdays back to myself so I could chill-out at home, but who was I kidding? After just a couple of weeks, I really missed the salon, and especially the girls. I started to look for another job, but wasn't interested in any of those on offer. A friend's mum knew someone who ran one of those household goods catalogues so the two of us gave it a go. So, we walked the roads near to where we lived pushing endless booklets through endless doors and if that wasn't mind numbing enough we had to go back a few days later to collect them. As neither of us had reached driving age yet we had no adequate form of transport so off we went on foot delivering orders. Now I think it's only fair that customers should expected their orders to arrive in pristine condition, but we had no love for the job and there is a limit to how many mops we could carry between us. We found the easiest way of delivery was to drag them by their heads to their destination. This proved to be a good idea although the ends of the aluminium poles didn't fare well on the ground and, by the time we had finished many needed to be sent back for replacements as the ends were scratched and looked ten years old and nothing but brand new. Predictably, we were both promptly dismissed of our duties, thank goodness!

Then the call came asking whether I would like to return on Saturdays to the salon as business had picked up again, but now I had the offer of an apprenticeship should I want it as I was soon to leave school. Of course, this I did without hesitation and I seized both opportunities. I couldn't help but ask if anyone had left in my absence and inevitably it was the only girl with whom I hadn't gelled. At the end of the day, she had brought it on herself: she never looked happy and was told many times to smile as it's such a big part of our job. Not only do you need to learn the skill of hairdressing, you also need to perfect the art of keeping how you feel from the clients. People come to us to relax and the presence of someone who looks unhappy around them doesn't make the customer feel good. No matter what's going on in your life it's not the client's problem and you just have to show a brave face and get on with it. Our faces can reveal many emotions and when this was pointed out to me it seemed an important skill to master. When you are working full time in a very people-orientated environment you can understand and appreciate the effect this can have on the clientele and your colleagues; just working alongside someone like that can really bring you down as time goes on. If you don't realise what you are doing and have it brought to your attention for your own benefit as well as everyone you come in to contact with please take notice and learn to smile before it's too late!

It wasn't long before my training began in earnest and I needed to start finding myself models on whom to practice: this is one of those times when you find out who your real friends are! I convinced my sister and friends that everything was supervised and put my life to it and so, with that they then did me the great favour of entering into a world of colour, restyles and perms.

Depending on where you undertake your apprenticeship you may also have the added experience of attending college. Some larger salon groups, *e.g.* Vidal Sassoon and Toni and Guy, have their own in-salon training and academies which teach their own unique methods and techniques. These larger training academies also open their doors to everyone and courses are always available to you at a cost, but most salons pay for or contribute towards them. So, with this in mind, you can learn and constantly update your skills from someone else's vision at any time you choose.

College is a valuable experience and perhaps the best way of attending is *via* 'Day Release', which usually means spending four days of the week in a salon and one day at college. By attending day release training, *i.e.* a two-year course, you are still able to receive your City and Guilds' certificate, which lists everything you have studied, completed and passed within your time there. Predominantly, it will show that you are qualified in cutting, perming and colouring hair, although other skills you have developed may be included as well. Over time, all this information builds up your professional portfolio, which is a real asset to present to future employers. They will see that not only are you qualified, but also that you have the ability to see something through to its conclusion.

You will find yourself mixing with people from other salons in the area and getting to know them can help you judge how well you are being treated, taught and paid by your employer. Hairdressing has always had a reputation for low pay until you are experienced, but with the advent of the minimum wage you are able to make sure you are getting what is rightfully yours.

I started out with a great teacher and this became very apparent to me once I attended practical lessons at college : I was always one of the few who were way ahead of most of the other students and I put this down to all the practical knowledge that I had received in the salon. Your employer has an obligation to your training: it's not simply about providing you with a job and making you clean all day, so again compare yourself with others and never be afraid to ask for the things to which you are entitled. Some salons do not allow you much 'hands on' work in the early days and this is a real shame, so for some students college really is the beginning.

We attended art, science, theory and practical lectures, all of which play a huge part in hairdressing. I'm sure that the inclusion of practical and theory speak for themselves, but you may be wondering why art and science? Art will help you to understand colour and really encourage your creative and visual instincts; science is important for the technical side of things (e.g. it will help you to understand how hair is structured as not all of it is visible to the naked eye).

I never really enjoyed school, but I attended my lessons because I knew it was the right thing to do. Art, geography, history and physical education were my favourite subjects. All involve self expression and, as with so many things, you can draw on these for inspiration. You only have to watch coverage of a volcano erupting and spewing lava, and become drawn in by the mighty power displayed by this phenomenon.

Fortunately, college did not entirely compare with school and I found it fairly light-hearted. I only had to attend for one day each week and was treated not so much as a pupil, but more of an adult. To attend full-time you will still need to offer some relevant exam grades to enrol on the course. However, if you are concerned that you will not do well in your exams at school then all is not lost, as you do not require any qualifications to attend via day release from a salon

Many people presume that full-time college is the best way to go, but I don't agree. If you are salon-based you receive much more hands on experience every day. Research your options, weigh everything up and make your own decisions, but don't be afraid to ask for advice. If you have a Saturday job in a salon ask the people there what worked for them, and if you aren't in a salon pop into one of your local hairdressers or ask the stylist who cuts your hair for some guidance, I'm sure they will be more than happy to help.

Don't get me wrong: I'm not suggesting that to attend college full-time is a bad thing - it's not. It's simply that I just found the advantages of working in a salon most of the week and attending college *via* `day release' gave me the best of both worlds. The only problem with going to college is the lack of `real' people upon whom you may practice on and, unless you have at least a Saturday job, you'll miss out on the true feel of busy daily salon life: day-by-day, week- in and week-out. Dealing with people all day and regularly will develop your salon skills and abilities and help you work as part of a team. This was something that worked wonders for me personally as I also thought that going full-time was the obvious way forward, but looking back now I am so pleased everyone at my salon talked me out of it. As I've said I was very lucky in the early days, I had a great teacher who had worked in many salons and had gained much experience and she also had a way about her which made things easy to understand. Practice hopefully makes perfect, but not everyone can grasp it.

Once or twice a year in-salon competitions are held and these really help you to monitor your progress. All though you should take these events seriously they are meant to be fun too, so nothing to lose sleep over just relax and do your best.

I believe strongly that many people take the view that, "It's only hair, so how hard can it be?" A comment often heard from non-hairdressers as they tend to view hairdressing as a lesser skill or profession. If only they knew what was involved, many wouldn't have the stamina to last the week! I honestly think the majority of good stylists have a natural talent which in the right hands can be developed to any degree as everything makes sense from the start and all natural patterns are obvious. On the other hand there are many people who love being part of the industry and who desperately want to succeed, but may never fulfil their potential. You will usually find they remain within their comfort zone: always turning out the same haircuts and sticking with their handful of favourite colours which they no through repetition makes the end result a safe one.

As the weeks went on I started to build-up a friendship with the girls especially Cath and Frank. We had a laugh together which made learning more fun. We got to a stage where they started inviting me to socialise with them outside of work; I accepted their offers and had a whale of a time. Frequently, I found myself in the pub. after work for a 'swift half', going on great nights out and having a ball. The worst night of the week to go out was Friday evening as almost everyone else would be out: for most it was the end of their working week. However, this does not apply to you if you choose a career in hairdressing, as all salons open on a Saturday and this usually tends to be one of the busiest days of the week. I, like millions of hairdressers worldwide have suffered many a time as a result of too many vodka oranges, that one double gin and tonic too many and of course that old favourite, "well I only had four glasses of wine, so I don't understand why I'm feeling so rough." I always managed to forget that they were large glasses of wine and that I had already had 'one or two' at home whilst getting ready. As the day went on and my head went even more downhill I would have a flashback of that tequila slammer I necked once in the night club before going on to churn it all up into one big cocktail in my stomach as Black Box's 'Ride on Time' came over the dance-floor. Unlike most, I was rarely sick, at least during the early years. As I got older I never could deal with it quite so well and when I was sick, I *really* was. Quite rightly I never received any sympathy from my mum and I remember her saying, "I don't know where you get it from. I hardly drink, your father hardly drinks, why can't you be more like your sister? She never comes home in these states!" I would convince myself that I would never drink again! That said, by the time the next weekend was upon us I would do it all over again.

Despite this, I never called in sick at work because I had partied too much the night before, which I believe was due in no small part to my upbringing. However bad I felt, I'd still turn up for work in the morning and get on with the day ahead, reasoning that how I was feeling was totally my own doing so why should my colleges suffer a harder day with me off sick? Moreover, if I were absent my colleagues' workloads would increase greatly and once I became a stylist I couldn't be responsible for letting down all my clients who liked me doing their hair. This is not meant to suggest that life in hair will turn you into a raging alcoholic, far from it. Many teenagers, no matter what they do in their lives and careers, will experiment with alcohol and many other substances I'm sure. Nevertheless, hairdressing can be a very social experience and one which will bring you many laughs, great memories and probably many new friends along the way.

The ability to get along with colleagues is vital as it can be a very solitary day if you don't learn to communicate with the people around you. I have worked alongside some extremely extroverted and very colourful beings: some that continuously wear their everyday heart and mood on their arm for all to see. Others on the other-hand can be so private or introverted that even after spending many hours a day, a week or even years in their company I still couldn't tell you a thing about them. This is rarely the best way to be: I have seen several colleagues throughout my career who have ended up isolating themselves to the point where others stop trying and give up including them in salon banter or inviting them on evenings out. If you are someone who takes time letting your guard down, are somewhat shy and in general prefer your own company, you really do need to take time to interact with people at work as it will have a huge impact on your status in the salon and very importantly your relationships with your much needed clientele. As much as your customers will love your approach to their crowning glory for many it is also your personality to which they become attracted.

As for myself, once around family and friends that I'd known for years I could always be heard laughing and joking and certainly holding my own. Yet put me in a new situation or environment where I knew nobody and I became a different person. I never thought of myself as shy, but in these areas I could be extremely quiet. I always took time to work people out and socialised only with those around whom I became comfortable. These days I can hear people saying, "you must be kidding, you quiet? NEVER! You must be referring to someone else". And I am: I left that person behind many years ago, but not intentionally. As time moved on I learnt to involve myself with many different types of people and found I'd fallen into a great social scene. Over the years I made many great friends, without some of whom my life's history would be quite unimaginable. As a result, I ended up a much more knowledgeable, understanding colourful and rounded person. Having some backbone and a sense of responsibility will serve you well. It will gain you respect and most probably take you a long way, hopefully bringing you what you desire from life. Many careers will help your confidence no end, but for me it was hairdressing and everything that goes with it that made me the person I am today and for that I am extremely thankful and very proud of how hard I have worked at embracing and developing that skill.

MEN AND MISTAKES

"*C*ongratulations, you are officially qualified". These words seemed to be a lifetime in coming, but were music to my ears. I had worked hard in the salon and at college: both of which had finally paid off. However, becoming qualified may mean one thing to you, but not quite the same thing to your employer. The problem rears its head when we qualify and naively assume that we are now going to make that big jump and leave the last two or three years' of washing peoples hair, passing-up perm rollers and foils cleaning the shelves and 'cleaning for cleaning's sake' well and truly behind us. Well think again!

I fully appreciate this frustration as I have obviously been there. Towards the end of your training and this happens to us all, you get a little disheartened. You will naturally become tired of your constant chores and convince yourself that you have done your time as 'Molly Maid', 'stick a broom up my ****, and I'll sweep the floor at the same time' apprentice and you now want a piece of the *real* action. The only thing holding you back is that you do not yet have a clientele. Whilst your employer knows that you want and need to move on, but this little blip takes time to build up. No employer wants his or her staff just sitting around we all have to do something to earn our wages and so, unfortunately, to begin with for the majority of us we have to carry on for a little longer with our chores. However, there will be light at the end of the salon as you should now start to take on the new clients that ring-up or walk through the door at short notice, as hopefully all the other stylists will be unable to accommodate, them as their columns should be full. So this leaves the door well and truly wide open for you to present yourself as the 'just popped in on the off chance' customer's brand new stylist, full of great ideas for her or him for many years to come.

As new stylist's we should appear keen to do anything, but so many of us seem to shy away from cutting men's hair. I did, as did most of the stylists I worked alongside. Why? The only reason I can think of is they are the opposite sex and they have a way of unconsciously unnerving us. We stop thinking as hairdressers and don't apply the obvious way of thinking, 'it's still hair' and go into 'oh no it's a man' mode. It is a funny reaction as most of us grew up with or around our fathers and lots of us have brothers, boyfriends or husbands, so what's the problem? They may not always shower enough, have strange dangly bits, snore like thunder and have the most unthinkable habits, but they aren't all aliens, are they? I was no exception - I too wanted to run a mile, but I stopped shying away from them and eventually you wonder what all the fuss is about. Guys started to ask for my name which you can usually take as a good sign as it normally means they like what you have done and intend to ask for you again! On the other hand they may just want to clarify who you are so not to get you again, but that really doesn't happen very often if you know you've done your job well. As usual everything is learnt through experience, but I still know girls even now who won't cut a man's hair and can be seen hurrying down the salon to hide if they are not doing anything when a guy enters the salon. You can hear the door shut as they rush into the toilet for cover or can be seen rummaging in the fridge for food so they can pretend to be on their lunch break (at only 10.30). If all this fails and there's no other option we hope for mercy and say, 'can't someone else do it? I'm scared!

Colour is an awesome part of hairdressing, so don't be scared of it; embrace it with both hands. It tends to be obvious if a client has colour in their hair. I find lots of people love partial colouring as in this way they can enjoy a great look without huge commitment. You will still have those who love the crazy colours, so don't think it will all become a little boring as each client will be different from the previous one. As far as mistakes go, I consider myself to have been fairly lucky over the years, although I'd like to think that there has been a huge chunk of knowledge and judgement in there too. Many a close call has needed some rapid reappraisal to be made and in some cases you need to think very quickly indeed where colour is concerned.

After I became qualified I was officially let loose with colour; I never thought I knew all that there was to know, but I was really caught out in the early days by the 'special blonde' colours (these are fairly light tones which clients often prefer over bleach). I remember one occasion particularly clearly. My client had fairly short hair and wanted to be blonde all over so I thought it shouldn't be a problem as people go blonde all the time. She wasn't that dark, only a medium natural blonde, but on the warm side as I remember. So off I went and applied a 'special blonde' all over her hair. As I kept an eye on its development I could see it starting to lift quite quickly which was great as she was a little late in the day to be having a colour. I should be able to cut it and still leave on time, or so I thought, unknown to me the colour had other ideas. When I returned after fifteen minutes it was all a mass of yellow, but at this stage I didn't panic too much as it still had the best part of half an hour to go. I knew what ash tones were and we had settled on the colour special ash blonde which both she and I liked. From the many times I had used it now and had observed other stylist's use this colour I was sure it would turn out a great success, but I was wrong... very wrong! Even if you have relatively dark hair 'high-lift' products still manage to achieve lift and are accompanied by other shades can create fabulous lighter tones throughout the hair. I had no problem with this as I had now carried-out many successful sets of what we call weaves or foils, but the problem I had was when applied as an all-over colour, unless the natural hair is predominately cool toned and doesn't carry much depth there is no getting away from the warmth the product generates from the hair's own natural colours. When coloured strands of hair lie alongside other shades, depths and tones they tend to complement each other and don't always appear so prominent compared to how they would as an individual colour occupying the whole head of hair. These lighter shades can still look rather golden, but do not show themselves to be dramatically this way when offset by other tones.

I had not yet been put in the position where a client wanted to be that light all over without using bleach so I didn't consider that my approach was about to become a huge dilemma. All my colours had looked great until now so I didn't foresee a problem here. I checked the development after fifteen minutes it was looking extremely yellow, but it can take up to forty five minutes to achieve the desired look so I wasn't too worried at this point. The client had noticed the obvious glow to her head, but I managed to convince her not to panic as this was relatively normal with some colour changes. I was doing everything text book style and I knew that in another twenty to thirty minutes all should be perfect and she would love me. A little later the lady asked me how everything was going: I informed her all was good and I would be washing it off soon and if it needed a toner which is quite normal I would pop it on at the basin. My heart was racing beyond belief and I'm sure she saw my face change colour as well as expression. I could tell she had worked out what I now had to admitted to myself - it wasn't going to get any better!

As we walked towards the basins all I could think of was running away. I wanted the ground to swallow me up so I didn't have to face this poor lady. What had I done? All she wanted me to do was give her a lovely blonde crop, but instead I had turned her into a canary! At this point, I had the feeling that most stylists have experienced at some point as my heart had well and truly left my torso and had now become firmly planted in my mouth. I soon became aware that my hands were shaking and I could barely speak, this really is one of the worst feelings ever. I washed off the colour, but to no avail and so I asked a couple of stylists for help. We applied a toner or three to help neutralise the gold which did help, but there was still lots of room for improvement. By this time the salon had sailed past closing time and I hadn't even cut the lady's hair yet, but something told me that she wouldn't want me to anyway.

I took her to the mirror so she could see the progress we had made. I could tell by the way a shaky hand lit up yet another cigarette (in those days you could smoke anywhere, even in the hairdressers), that she was in shock and she didn't say much but her eyes were welling up. At this point all I could hear myself saying was, "I'm sorry, I'm so sorry". I guess I was fortunate that she didn't scream the salon down and somehow I knew she would not return the next day for the highlights we planned to put in to break-up all that yellow, and she didn't. Every day for over a week I kept expecting her to turn up in reception and go bananas but I never saw her again. I felt terrible for my lack of knowledge that day, but unfortunately mistakes such as these help us to learn and become something really good in time.

I remember the time I got my bowls of colour mixed up and put the copper red on my client's white roots and the natural soft brown in the foils which evidently were nowhere to be seen after being washed off, but the roots seemed so bright they could have directed the ships in. I am certainly not proud of mistakes like these and, when you are working with a large team, situations like these will make your colleagues curl up laughing as they see you panic to near death. However, once they have got themselves back under control they will usually help out and that is one of the great comforts of working in a salon environment.

Colour is a wonderful asset; like paint is to an artist. Earn your clients' trust and they will become a blank canvas for you to reinvent time and time again. Find out through a great consultation what your client would like from you that day; maybe introduce a few ideas of your own and, coupled with the ability to listen, you will be sure to gain your client's confidence. I love the way colour can really reinvent your look. As certain times of the year start or draw to a close this is where a hairdresser can gather much inspiration: summer is a great time for experimenting with lighter brighter shades. Most of us have a certain colour we like the idea of, but can be scared to take that step. If it is summer blondes look great by staying bright and vivacious with flashes of bleach for brilliance or more caramel tones to create depth especially to finer hair. Both brunettes and redheads benefit from the right choice of highlights so you've got something for everyone. When you are on holiday study the sand and the way the light reflects off the water. If you use your creative mind these things should help to feed your imagination and you can reflect them in your work. Autumn is another great time to help make sure the winter blues are kept at bay: again look at what is happening around you and take it into the salon. The summer often ends with a build-up of chlorine, tangles and split ends so why not take this opportunity to surprise your clients with yet some more great ideas? Tame those sun-bleached blondes by offering a choice of warmer honey tones, or be brave and suggest a mixture of toffee and chocolate shades or vibrant reds and plums.

Although I am talking colour here, there is room just to mention products as they are a huge industry. Not only will you be learning how to cut, colour and style hair you will also need to teach people how to create, maintain and protect their look. Split ends don't repair naturally and heavy overgrown layers will not suddenly revive themselves overnight. They both will benefit from a haircut, but you can introduce products to aid your work and help keep problems at bay. You must understand the principles of caring for hair and teach this to your clients. When you think about it what is the point of allowing them to spend all that money on a great cut and fabulous colour if all you are going to do is let them starve it of vital care. You will not be able to convince everyone to buy the correct products, but you will be surprised at how many of your clients do want to do the right thing and protect their latest investment. You will learn about all the best shampoos, conditioners, treatments, reconstructive technology and all the styling products you could ever imagine and believe me there are a lot out there. They all promise to protect and condition, add body, movement, sculpt and hold to whatever degree you desire, but not every product will work for everyone and every style so it's down to you to do your homework and decide what will work best for your clients and they will trust you to give them the best advice.

Another avenue to explore if you fancy being out and about is becoming a sales representative. Every company needs them to get their name and products out there. This can mean a lot of doors being closed in your face as many salon owners are not interested in change or are very happy with what they already stock. If you like a challenge, have broad shoulders and think you can sell anything to anyone then somewhere down the line this could be for you.

HERE TODAY; GONE TOMORROW

I have often wondered what life working on a cruise ship would have to offer. Not something I entered into in the end, but I did contact a couple of the well known companies for some advice. Many hairdressers decide that after several years of working on land a life at sea could be for them. It's not just the Navy that sets sail around the world, you could do too. For many years, people have enjoyed relaxing, holidaying, partying and generally living their life on the crest of a wave. Years ago, the most glamorous of lifestyles onboard ship were reserved for the rich and famous but not anymore; these days the cruise has become more affordable and for those with that dreaded fear of flying it really is a godsend. As with any great night out on the town or that special occasion, sea-goers need their hair done too. All the cruise liners have an on board salon that aims to cater for the needs of their guests. Themed nights, parties or simply going for dinner usually requires a certain dress code and most, especially women, love an excuse to 'go to town'. Now this doesn't just stop with a new dress and pair of heels, it has to be the whole package or it isn't worth the effort …and this is where you come in. All these ladies need their hair attending to, to complete their look. Many of the clients on ship will require you to wash and blow-dry their hair so as to look more groomed for the evening or put their hair up for a more 'chic' approach. As there will be many passengers on board requesting your skills some stylists may find this life very repetitive yet others may never tire of night after night of the very similar requests. Remember that work is work wherever you are in the world and even though this lifestyle can all appear very champagne and sparkle, for the majority of the trip this is for the customers and you will get your time to relax and have fun when all the hard work is done. The ship will always have a destination so you and your colleges will get some time to yourselves to explore and chill-out before everyone back on board and off to the next port of call. It can be a great way to spend your working day, the choice is yours and maybe for those of you who find it hard to in one place for too long this could be a great move for you so why not give it some thought?

If this lifestyle is appealing to you, you will probably need to get yourself experienced on land first and have an understanding of putting hair up. Learning this art is a wonderful and very creative skill and to execute it with perfection you will have that creative streak already within you or lots of practice will help make perfect. Like anything creative there is only so much you can be taught, the rest either comes naturally or it doesn't. In my experience, hair up was hardly touched upon in college and rarely received that much coverage within salon training sessions. Most of the people I have worked alongside of have practiced at home on friends or just got better with time through trial and error within the salon. All is not lost though as there are some great courses out there that you can book yourself on to in order to learn from the best in this field. I have been to several shows where such people flaunt their talent and I have

always left feeling blown away by their extensive imagination. Putting hair up for whatever the occasion was just something with which I could never really get to grips, you can't be good at everything and this wasn't for me. Although I do wish that there had been more encouragement to try it when I started out as I would have loved to have seen what I may have been able to achieve, but my career snowballed fairly quickly in the early years and as time went on, there never seemed to be enough time for me to learn. Make sure you get everything that is available to you and if it isn't then make it available as the earlier you start learning the better you will become. Try looking in hair magazines, the Hairdresser's Journal or contact the local college, look online as everything you will ever need is probably listed there somewhere.

With lots of the right experience under your belt you will be ready for your new life at sea. For many people the best time to enter into this side of a hairdressing career would probably be when you are free and single as that way you will not have any ties or commitments on land which may hinder your life away from home. Once you are in a steady relationship or married with children it may prove a lot harder to be away from your home and family for several days or weeks at a time. The great thing about a life in hairdressing is how transportable it is; you can travel the world with this trade and you will never be short of work. British hairdressing is viewed worldwide as second to none with students travelling from all over to study at one of the many outstanding academies we have to offer in order to gain a great education. We are in great demand to leave our motherland and take our scissors across the globe to countries as far afield as Australia to share our knowledge. The world really is your oyster and there really are some fantastic opportunities out there for you all under one trade.

BACKACHE, HEADACHE, HEARTACHE

$\mathcal{A}$ friend's sister had just moved back to England and was starting up an aerobics class in the local hall on a Thursday night. She asked me if I fancied going along to the class to keep her company, keep fit and give her sister some support. I was only sixteen and didn't drive so I walked everywhere. I was as skinny as a rake: looked myself up and down and couldn't see anything wrong with me, but did understand the importance of keeping fit and healthy. I decided that it was something I would love to get into and although I didn't need to exercise for my weight I knew it would be great for my overall health.

Thursday came and I dashed home after work to get myself ready for the big aerobics session. Little did I know at the time, but exercise was about to become a regular event for me and would feature greatly in my life over the years to come. As we pulled up in the car park, giggling as usual, the doors were already open ready to greet the 'keep fitters' in the neighbourhood. I could hear my friend's sister shouting, "Come on ladies let's all get our mats on the floor and our bodies warmed up and ready to go". Making sure she could be heard over Madonna's 'Like a Prayer' funky dance mix she led us straight into a routine. Right from the start I knew I was going to enjoy it and I did. At the end of the class I said I intended to go regularly as I thought it was great fun, although the next day was a different story. I woke up feeling fine until I decided to get out of bed, it was agony! I walked the mile to work every day and believe me this particular morning my calf muscles had something to complain about. We kept up with the classes and eventually the sore legs and aching thighs came to an end, although I have to admit that even now if I try a new sport or activity I still find the odd muscle I didn't know I had.

As I continued to learn through the years of Hairdressing I also continued learning the importance of health and fitness. Your health is and will always be your rock in life. With it you have the ability to do absolutely anything you wish, but without it you may struggle to achieve your goals. So many people ascend to great heights by overcoming their health issues and disabilities and they are true champions, but to let such a precious thing as your general health and well being slip through your fingers is a selfish act and for this you will only have yourself to hold responsible and probably suffer the consequence at some point in your life.

Over the years I have attended many different types of exercise classes ranging from aerobics, step aerobics, body combat, spinning (a stationary cycling class), sessions in the gym horse riding and running. All these classes you may have noticed, involve a fair amount of energy on my part, but even on days where you hardly have any to spare, once you finish a session you feel so much better and will be pleased with yourself for making the effort. Taking regular exercise I believe really does contribute greatly to your wellbeing in the long term if you should be seriously considering a career in hairdressing.

Stamina is probably the main issue for you in hairdressing. To be able to complete on a regular basis the long days of continual standing you can't be without it and stamina is achieved by focus, perseverance and dedication. In the early days you will probably be shattered every night and your legs will ache along with your back and shoulders. I have been aware many times over the years how students 'cave in' and give up within a very short space of time and in a couple of cases they have thrown in the towel (no pun intended) after the first day! Now sympathy where sympathy's due, but I'm not a very sympathetic person in this type of situation. I was brought up to work hard and not to expect everything to be handed to me and that is one of the many great assets you can have instilled into you from those early teenage years. If you can't handle a hard day's work especially when it is all in your favour and many great talents are waiting in the wings in your salon to lend you all their knowledge and expertise for free, then quite frankly our industry doesn't need you.

It isn't just the physical aspects with which exercise will help you, it's the mental side of things too. When you work in a people-orientated environment every day you will encounter many different characters. Dealing with the majority isn't going to prove to be an impossible task, but there will be a few clients or staff members who will put your patience to the test big time and some will revel in doing so. To me exercise helps to clear your mind of daily stresses and strains, *e.g.* when I run or cycle I need to concentrate on my rhythm to keep me going. I find that by thinking through any confusions or encounters that I have struggled with that day really helps to drive me and by the end of the session my mind is more at ease and a lot of the stress or frustration has burnt away. The thought of pounding the streets won't always be appealing to everyone and many people take solace in more relaxing therapies. Yoga and Pilates are great favourites also; Thai Chi and many other forms of martial arts are just as beneficial and will train the mind as well as the body. Stress in my eyes is a form of poison to our well being and although none of us can go through life avoiding it completely, some of us will unfortunately encounter much more than our fair share. By keeping a fit body and a healthy mind you should be able to tackle life's challenges a little easier, whether in or out of the salon.

I have worked extremely hard in my career especially as the manageress of someone else's business. I have therefore suffered many a backache or `headache' over the years as you can imagine. The former is predominately work related and the latter, if not brought on by women's monthly issues, the in-salon music being too loud or our old favourite the weather, is frequently caused by a member of staff. "Why", I have asked myself for years, "is it that rules and regulations are set out and upheld by

all the other salon members yet there is always the one that feels she or
he is exempt?" It drives me, and I am sure many others, to distraction! I
have been heard talking to myself many times around the salon: "If I have
to tell her one more time" or "God give me strength". Then there's, "I will
surgically remove her from that stool and stick it where..." These people
don't realise how much their actions affect the people around them as it
is extremely disrespectful to your fellow colleges and peers. The need to
repeat yourself continually covering the same issues eventually becomes
totally mind-numbing and those people create you one big headache. I
am positive that most employers or managers do not enjoy nagging at
their staff continuously over trivial issues so stop making us!

Managing people as well as making sure the day–to-day running of a
very popular salon goes as smoothly as possible is no easy task, especially
in the early days. When such a role is given to you, I was about twenty-
five at this point, you gladly receive it as by this stage in your career you
believe you have earned and deserve this title and I was no exception. I
had proven I was more than capable of keeping my head in dealing with
difficult situations and regaining calm to potentially stressful areas. On
many occasions, with the aid of a couple of helpful members of the
team, I had got stuck into rebooking, reorganising or unfortunately
cancelling one, two or sometimes even three stylists columns when a
Saturday proved too much for them when they were genuinely ill or quite
possibly hung-over. All this would take place before we started work on
our own clients' needs that day. Sometime further down the line, when
the glory has worn off, you will probably see management as more of a
curse than a trophy and contemplate handing the job back in favour of
your original role. The thing you need to remember about a career in
hairdressing is that just because the sign on the door says closed it doesn't
mean to suggest you're going home. More often than not, I found myself
shutting up shop and finally going home the best part of an hour after
most of the other staff. Why? Well to begin with hair doesn't always do
what it should as colours may take longer to develop than first thought,
or it only takes for a client to turn up late at some point in the day and

this can throw your whole day out of kilter, causing you to run behind schedule for the rest of your clients. You have to remember that whatever happens to you can also happen to all the other stylists, so if you accept the title of manager you have to accept what goes with it. Frequently I had finished my work and duties, but another stylist might had been over-running - unfortunately you can't simply ask a customer to return to the salon another day for their hair to be completed so you, or they, must keep going until it is. And then there is still the matter of cashing up at the end of the day and if the till doesn't balance you may be there a long time making sure it does and one of the biggest responsibilities in managing someone else's business is the money. I know it cannot always be avoided, but in my experience there shouldn't be too many people using the till. I do not imply any distrust, but it is simply that anyone can make a mistake: too much, or too little change can be given for payment , or when busy talking or getting caught up making other appointments it can be very easy to forget to charge at all.

Throughout the year you will face many a demanding day, for one reason or another, and I can think of many a time that I took my lunch to work with me and ended-up taking it back home again as there really wasn't the time to stop and eat it. In my experience even if you had a break set out for you if a client wanted an appointment your break was cancelled. I am not saying that this is the case in all salons, just that it can be a downside to working in a busy salon or one that fails to understand the importance of a decent break or that food will fuel the staff and they will run more efficiently. Frequently, clients asked, "have you had lunch?" As thoughtful as this may sound not many made you feel you could do it on their time, but it was more than okay for me to keep the next customer waiting.

If you didn't have them before you certainly will have broad shoulders as your managerial role develops. Maybe you are the type of person that always seems to attract other people's problems, or perhaps you are a good listener? Even if this is not you, you will need to learn the art of listening, understanding and dealing with others upsets and dilemmas.

What may seem ridiculous or petty to you can be a huge deal to someone else. As we get older we experience many different struggles and upheavals, but just as a divorce, death or personal problem may be a huge demand on you in your thirties, forties, or fifties, *etc.*, breaking up with a boyfriend, when the member of staff may only be sixteen, is just as important to that individual, as everything is relevant at a certain stage in life. The position will require a certain amount of compassion, understanding and patience on your part to fulfil this role to the maximum and the best of your ability. All this, along with treating people fairly and without favouritism will, in turn, gain you the respect of your colleagues making it so much easier for you to carry out your role efficiently and with the support of your team. With everyone getting on well the day runs smoother for all involved. You must learn to delegate as it's all too much for one person; if others have responsibilities they will probably feel much more part of the team and more valid within the salon. By trying to do everything yourself, as well as working a full day as a stylist, you will run yourself completely into the ground and end up of little use to anyone.

One of the busiest times of the year for us, and a favourite of mine, is Christmas time. It is said to be the time for giving and receiving, but

I can't help but think that they missed out the word 'finding': finding the time to fit everything in, or for we busy hairdressers finding enough appointments in the day for all our clients. Now, especially for we ladies, it may be good luck that our next six-week appointment falls at Christmas, or we juggle the weeks around so as to fit in that extra colour ready for all those parties, but let's face it most of us want to look great for Santa. Whatever the reason or occasion and be it 'hair up', 'hair down', 'hair up with some down', 'hair coaxed in to tumbling stresses', or the simplicity of the 'silky and smooth' we really do need to keep our heads at a very hectic and demanding time in the social calendar.

By accepting the title and role of manageress I knew my skills and attributes had not gone unnoticed, but I soon learnt that with promotion came jealousy. A couple of staff members, who were not up to the job yet didn't like me being promoted above them, decided to make life harder for me. Some would get their kicks from trying to intimidate me by making fun of me or imitating me to create laughs with the weaker members of the team as they knew they had no backbone to ignore them. Others with stronger characters found that it was amusing to become the loudest voice in order to undermine my confidence and try to gain some laughs and status at my expense. On many occasions, I was left to deal with, cancel and rearrange many a client due to the actions of those who thought it funny to try and wind me up continually throughout the morning and then, when they inevitably came to realise the joke had worn thin as I had not broken down or given in, the only way to deal with defeat would be to scream at me across the salon and walk out in a very dramatic Oscar-deserving departure. On the other hand, I had a job to do: by not rising to the bait I always emerged with my dignity and self respect intact.

Unfortunately, in my late twenties I suffered the loss of my mother, a lovely lady who tragically persevered to battle a medical mistake, but as time went on that battle was lost and, as they say, life goes on. Well yes it did for the world around me, but I went into my own world. For a long time, I continued on 'auto pilot': getting up for work, going out with friends, and generally getting on, but a huge part of me died too. Many people wear their hearts on their sleeves, but that's not me. I would always tell everyone that I was fine, as there didn't seem anything they could do and no amount of talking about it or wishing would bring her back. I went on the rampage for some time, enjoying life to the maximum and ridding it of all things that I knew were not right for me anymore. I divorced my erstwhile husband, a lovely man, but the relationship was not how I intended the rest of my life to be. Death helps you to evaluate life and drums into you that this is the only chance you are going to have, so get it right and, if it's not then as it seems, then don't put up with it, have the courage to deal with it and move on. Believe me, it may take some time, but you will end up so much happier in the long term. Throughout these events, which spanned several years, and without my realising it, I had many people around watching over me. These people worked alongside me every day and somehow they did a great job of keeping me sane. When I look back I can't help but think that, had I of chosen a career which involved spending my time shut away in an office alone for the majority of the day with my own thoughts, I might not have moved forward from this emotional roller coaster as well as I did. At my lowest point the doctor prescribed medication although, while I'm not saying that it's wrong, far from it, a life of anti-depressants was not for me. I believe that time is a great healer and I needed to deal with my sadness, fears and heartache rather than cover them up, otherwise I would never begin to heal. Having so many great colleges and real friends around me at that time, picking me up, making me laugh and on some days even making sure I ate properly, really did help get me through my heartache and distress during such a tough time in my life and I will always remember those people.

I credit hairdressing for not only uncovering a talent which I love, but for also introducing me to some of my now closest and dearest friends. As we grow up, go to college, work, travel, and leave home, we leave a lot of our primary friends behind us. This is not always intentional just part of life's course. I have few that I call great friends, people who I can truly trust and to whom I can open up, but that's just me: I can be quite a closed book. However, throughout what became many years of working in a salon environment I was surrounded by an array of lovely people whom I know respected me for the person I am and hopefully trusted me to work in their best interests knowing I was always loyal to them. I once heard it stated that staff should perhaps be scared or frightened of their employer; I found this extremely ridiculous and in some ways quite comical as whoever wishes to trade in these terms will surely have very little if any respect from their employees and an inharmonious and negative atmosphere within their salon. I did, I hope, always try to see matters from both sides of the salon rather than just doing what may have been expected of me as a manager. I don't believe for one minute that good management is a question of whose side you are on (management or staff), but more about achieving the best for both.

I LOVE WHAT I DO, BUT WHAT NOW?

How many of us at some point in our lives will think about starting a family? Most sensible adults will try to do the right thing by planning this new chapter in our lives for what is termed 'the right time.' We will spend time working out if we can afford this new addition as babies don't come cheap and one of us, usually the mother, will have to take time off work to look after the new arrival.

I remember saying, "I'm pregnant", in a very controlled quiet voice. I sounded in control of everything else in my life even if really I wasn't so why should this announcement be any different? We had only been trying for a couple of months: suddenly this was it and the rest of our lives were now committed to putting someone else first; we were no longer the most important people. I had met and married the love of my life, a man for whom most things except getting up in the morning seemed to be relatively easy once he put his mind to them. "If you work hard enough in life you will get what you deserve", he will say and, just this once, I will let him be right.

At seven and a half months pregnant and at a local restaurant I suddenly found myself in labour, not exactly what I had ordered as I had just sat down ready to tuck in to my evening meal. It was Friday night and I was staring longingly at the glass of wine I allowed myself at the end of each week, but looking back now had we of realised I was in the early stages of labour my dear friend's would have known that unless Chianti possessed the same strengths as an epidural, having a little sip each time I gripped the table when a wave of pain left me breathing like a nuisance caller just wasn't going to help! I love my food and so I cleared the plate before considering calling the hospital for advice. I made it home and once in my favourite penguin pyjamas with a hot water bottle between my legs for comfort I was able to think straight. I truly thought that if I could just go to sleep all would be fine in the morning; at midnight the ambulance arrived and at twenty past three in the afternoon of Monday twentieth October our son Danny was born.

So what happens now? I want to be a good mother, but I can't let all those years of hard work just disappear. And what about the clients that had become so loyal to me for all those years I didn't want to let them down and abandon them just like that. My son was in special care for some time as he was too premature to be out in the big wide world with his mum and dad so I had lots of time to think. I decided I no longer wanted to be in a salon situation under someone else's regime; I wanted to be with my son and working for myself. In common with many people I had no outside help with Danny and so for this to work I needed to always be available for my baby. My husband's suggestion to convert our garage into a 'mini salon' sounded the perfect solution, and equipped with a baby monitor, I

was able to run my very own business and still be able to hear his every sound should he awake. My clients, or friends as they had become, were fantastic, always understanding of my new situation and always ready to sneak a cuddle or bounce him on their knee. I always felt guilty about the clients I could no longer keep in contact with: I felt that I had let them down. However, there was only one of me and I now had someone else who depended on me, physically I could do no more. I felt extremely fortunate to have a working motherhood made more accessible to me, but even so it is the most tiring and challenging thing I have ever done.

Not everyone can give up their garage in this way or may not have a spare room in their house to convert for this purpose so many stylists allow their clients to come to their home with hair already washed so they can sit in the kitchen to have their hair done. Many stylists do extremely well for themselves running their own mobile business: a car is a must in this situation to enable you to transport all your equipment from one house to another. Once you have become fully qualified, and you have some wheels to see you on your way, you will be good to go. Many clients love a home visit as they don't have to worry what to do with the children while you are dealing with their hair, nor does their husband need to worry about getting booked into a salon at the last minute when he's left it too late. This way you can take on the whole family, brilliant! A great way to build up your clientele and what could be easier?

With so much going for it, it comes as no surprise that hairdressing really is a fabulous career to pursue. Introducing you to a world of glamour, fashion, all the latest make-up ideas and not to mention the opportunity to set up your very own business or to travel the world representing your country.

As the years have rolled on I can honestly look back and say that unless I had worked for a charity, become a nurse or carer or maybe even a vet there is no other career I could have chosen to obtain greater job satisfaction. It may have taken many years of perseverance, becoming a mother and my own boss, but on a working day I have always had my lunch no later than one thirty!

HOW TO BECOME A HAIRDRESSER

Getting started

It is fortunate for the budding hairdresser based in the U.K. that the career now has a recognised entry route involving either an N.V.Q. (national vocational qualification) or a S.V.Q. (Scottish vocational qualification) and these are the only qualifications recognised by employers in the U.K.

So what is an N.V.Q.?

Classed as an 'active qualification', this is truly vocational as you will learn by working and studying at the same time. Modern day apprenticeships are often the way forward in hairdressing, which involve regular assessment throughout your training. Through this route, you will work in a salon and attend college regularly (usually one day a week). The N.V.Q. syllabus will set out what is expected of you and what you need to complete to achieve your learning outcomes. Furthermore, it will list what you have to achieve at each stage in order to progress. Everything you do is focused on obtaining your N.V.Q. or S.V.Q. certificate and ultimately towards becoming a fully qualified hairdresser.

The N.V.Q. is set out in different levels; forming a solid foundation with the basic techniques and working your way up to more challenging tasks.

N.V.Q. level 1
- Shampooing
- Conditioning
- Drying hair
- Perming
- Colouring
- Health and safety

N.V.Q. level 2
- Cutting ladies' and men's hair
- Perming and colouring hair
- Drying and styling hair
- Client consultation
- Shampooing and conditioning
- Health and safety
- Shaving and massage

N.V.Q. 3
- Advanced techniques for cutting styling and drying hair
- Advanced colouring, perming and relaxing hair
- Financial management
- Training and assessing
- Teamwork
- Promotional work
- Salon development

At this point, you might have some additional questions...

Do you have to do an apprenticeship?

In short, 'no, you don't'. You may choose to study at college as a full time student, where you will undertake practical and theory lessons to gain qualifications.

If I choose an apprenticeship what are the benefits?

Undertaking an apprenticeship enables your employer to watch you work. They will observe how you develop over the next two or three years and see how you gel with others working in a team. An employer will get to know you: your strengths and weaknesses. You will gain greater experience in the day-to-day running of a salon and deal with many types of customers within the salon's clientele. An employer is more likely to offer a position to someone with hands-on experience and if you are already working in a salon as an apprentice your employer is more likely to offer you a job as a stylist at the end of your apprenticeship. One of the great benefits in an apprenticeship will be the opportunity to earn money! This way you can earn while you learn, what could be better?

How do I become an apprentice?

Take a look at the salons in your area. Pop in for some advice or ask whether they have, or will have, any jobs available. As the new college year starts in September, start looking early to avoid disappointment. Always leave your details, that way you can be contacted when they start enrolling.

Always look the part. Make sure your hair is clean and groomed as first impressions will make an impact. Apply make-up and dress with a sense of fashion as hairdressing is the whole package; when working you will become a walking advertisement. You will be interviewed by the salon owner or manager to detect your suitability to the industry.

What if I cannot find a salon with a vacancy?

Should you find yourself in this situation contact the 'national apprenticeships' helpline' (Tel. 0800 150600) they are there to help you. When you finish training and receive your qualifications there is still so much to learn. Keep yourself up to date as your career develops with the many courses available outside of college. Go online and check-out the well established academies such as Vidal Sassoon, Toni and Guy, Saks, Schwarzkopf, Loreal and Wella. Most of these offer one-, two- or three-day courses, which do come at a price - hopefully paid for by your salon, although some employers may not be in a position to cover this expense. Some travelling will be involved to get you to the academies: the trains, underground, buses and taxis get you pretty much to the door. This 'time out' can be a refreshing break from the salon, most students return revived and ready to show off their new material.

How do I get all my equipment?

Your employer and college will inform you of all the appropriate combs, scissors and brushes, *etc.* that you will need to get you started. They may order the equipment for you or advise you what to ask for at the wholesalers; either way it is usually your responsibility to pay for the purchases. You will need to take your equipment to work or college with you every day as all the tools of your trade will be needed for practical sessions, training days/evenings or if you should be called on to help-out on a busy day. Furthermore, it is down to you to look after your equipment and keep it clean.

The working week

It is extremely rare to find a salon that does not open on a Saturday: the big day in the working week when it is usually 'all hands on deck'. For many people, work commitments will mean that they can only make an appointment for this day - so you need to be available. As with so many businesses in the service industry, many salons have now begun to open on Sundays as well. These are usually worked out on a rota system so you won't be required to work on this day every week. You should expect to work a five day week with a day out to attend college. Some students have to use their day off to attend college, but most employers are gracious enough to understand that everyone needs a day to recharge their batteries.

Salon hours

Salons may open from eight o'clock in the morning to catch the early bird, whilst others may not open their doors until much later on certain days of the week. However, if this is the case you may end up finishing late on these days. Almost every salon will stay open late on at least one evening per week; this service helps clients who work in the daytime, so expect to work until seven, eight or nine o'clock at least one night of the week.

Working abroad

Look online as all the information you will need is there. For instance, countries such as Australia value great hairdressing skills. It is a fabulous trade to posses so let it help you see some of the world. When applying to work abroad your spoken English will need to be of a good standard and you will need several years' experience in both ladies' and men's hairdressing. You will need to have a rounded knowledge, usually encompassing a good technical ability in colour.

Lightning Source UK Ltd.
Milton Keynes UK

172953UK00001B/40/P